Romeo and Juliet

WILLIAM SHAKESPEARE

ADAPTED BY

Tom Gorman

SADDLEBACK
PUBLISHING·INC.

SADDLEBACK *Classics*

Hamlet

Julius Caesar

Macbeth

The Merchant of Venice

A Midsummer Night's Dream

Othello

Romeo & Juliet

The Tempest

Development and Production: Laurel Associates, Inc.
Cover and Interior Art: Black Eagle Productions

SADDLEBACK
PUBLISHING·INC.
Three Watson
Irvine, CA 92618-2767

Website: www.sdlback.com

Copyright © 2003 by Saddleback Publishing, Inc. All rights reserved. No part of this book may be reproduced in any form or by any means, electronic or mechanical, including photocopying, recording, or by any information storage and retrieval system, without the written permission of the publisher.

ISBN 1-56254-625-2

Printed in the United States of America
09 08 07 06   9 8 7 6 5 4 3 2 1

CONTENTS

CAST OF CHARACTERS

Montague family and friends:

ROMEO MONTAGUE: A young man

LORD MONTAGUE: Romeo's father and the enemy of Lord Capulet

LADY MONTAGUE: Romeo's mother

MERCUTIO: Romeo's friend and Prince Escalus's cousin

BENVOLIO: A cousin and friend to Romeo

BALTHASAR: Romeo's servant

ABRAHAM: Lord Montague's servant

FRIAR LAWRENCE: A Franciscan priest

FRIAR JOHN: An associate of Friar Lawrence

Capulet family and friends:

JULIET CAPULET: A 13-year-old girl

LORD CAPULET: Juliet's father and the enemy of Lord Montague

LADY CAPULET: Juliet's mother

NURSE: Juliet's nanny

SAMPSON and **GREGORY:** Servants to Lord Capulet

TYBALT: Juliet's cousin

PARIS: A young man who wants to marry Juliet; Prince Escalus's cousin

PRINCE ESCALUS: Prince and ruler of Verona

THE PROLOGUE

*(The **Chorus** enters.)*

CHORUS: Two families in Verona, Italy,
  equally respected,
  Have been feuding for many years.
  A daughter of one family and
  A son of the other—
  A pair of star-crossed lovers—
  Take their own lives.
  Their pitiful, needless deaths
  Bury their parents' feud.
  The sad story of their death-marked love
  And how it ended their parents' rage
  Is the subject of this play. If you listen well,
  Our play will fill in the details.

ACT 1

Scene 1

*(A street in Verona. **Sampson** and **Gregory** enter.
They are armed with swords.)*

SAMPSON: I tell you, Gregory, I won't be
  insulted by any of those Montague dogs!
GREGORY: Calm down, Sampson. Remember,
  The fight is between our masters—not us.

SAMPSON: It's all the same to me. I would go to the wall against any of them.

GREGORY: Well, you're about to get your chance. Draw your sword. Servants of the Montagues are coming now.

SAMPSON *(drawing his sword)*: Pick a fight with them. I'll back you up.

GREGORY: How? Turn your back and run?

SAMPSON: Fear not.

GREGORY: I'm more afraid of what *you* will do than I am of the Montagues.

SAMPSON: Let's keep the law on our side. Let them start it.

GREGORY: I will frown as I pass by. Let them take it as they will.

SAMPSON: Or as they dare! I will thumb my nose at them. They will lose face if they stand for it.

*(**Abraham** and **Balthasar** enter.)*

ABRAHAM: Do you thumb your nose at us, sir?

SAMPSON *(aside to Gregory)*: Is the law on our side if I say yes?

GREGORY: It is not.

SAMPSON: Then no, sir, I do not thumb my nose at you. But I do thumb my nose.

GREGORY: Do you want to fight, sir?

ABRAHAM: Fight? No, sir!

SAMPSON: Well, if you do, I am ready. I serve as good a man as you do.

ABRAHAM: As good, perhaps. But no better.

GREGORY: Say "better." Here comes Benvolio. He'll back us up.

SAMPSON: Yes, say *better*, sir.

ABRAHAM: You lie.

SAMPSON: Draw your swords, if you are men. Gregory, are you ready?

*(They fight. **Benvolio** enters.)*

BENVOLIO: Stop, fools! Put up your swords. You don't know what you're doing.

*(He beats down their swords. **Tybalt** enters.)*

TYBALT: Benvolio, do you fight with servants? Turn and get ready to die!

BENVOLIO: I'm just trying to keep the peace. Put your sword away— Or use it to help me stop this fight.

TYBALT: What? Your sword's drawn, And you talk of peace? I hate the sword, As I hate hell, all Montagues, and you! Come on, coward!

*(They fight. Others, from both sides, join in. Then **Lord and Lady Capulet** enter.)*

7

CAPULET: What's this? Give me a sword, too!

LADY CAPULET: A crutch is more like it!
Why do you call for a sword?

CAPULET: My sword, I say! Old Montague
Is coming and waving his blade to spite me.

(Lord and Lady Montague enter.)

MONTAGUE: You villain, Capulet!
(to his wife, who is holding him back): Let me go!

LADY MONTAGUE: No! Not one foot to seek a foe!

(Prince Escalus enters, with attendants.)

PRINCE: Rebels, enemies to peace,
Killers of your own neighbors—listen!

Throw down your weapons.
Hear the sentence of your angry prince.
Three fights between your two families
Have disturbed the quiet of our streets.
If you ever disturb our streets again,
You shall pay with your lives.
For now, clear the streets!
You, Capulet, shall go along with me.
And, Montague, you come this afternoon
To hear what I have to say about this case.
Once more, on pain of death, all men leave.

*(**Everyone** exits but Lord and Lady Montague and Benvolio.)*

MONTAGUE: Who started this fight, nephew?

BENVOLIO: Capulet's servants and yours
Were fighting hand to hand when I got here.
I drew my sword to part them. Just then,
Tybalt came, with his sword out.
He swung it about and cut the winds, which,
Not being hurt, hissed at him in scorn.
As we were trading blows, more and more
People joined in the fight.
Then the prince came and stopped it.

LADY MONTAGUE: Oh, where is Romeo?
Did you see him today?
I am glad he was not in this fight.

BENVOLIO: Madam, an hour before the sun
Peered from the golden window of the east,

My troubled mind drove me to take a walk.
I saw your son in a grove of sycamores.
I walked toward him, but he saw me
And stole away into the woods.
I could see that he wanted to be alone,
So I did not follow him.

MONTAGUE: He has been seen there often,
Adding tears to the fresh morning's dew.
But as soon as the sun begins to rise,
My son goes home to escape the light.
He locks himself in his room and
Shuts his windows, keeping fair daylight out
And making himself an artificial night.
If he would only tell us what is wrong,
We would do anything we could to help.

BENVOLIO: Well, here he comes.
I'll see if I can find out anything.

MONTAGUE: I hope you can.
(to Lady Montague): Come, madam, let's go.

(Lord and Lady Montague exit. Romeo enters.)

BENVOLIO: Good morning, cousin.

ROMEO: Is the day so young?
Ah, me! Sad hours drag on so!
Was that my father who just left?

BENVOLIO: It was. What sorrow makes your
hours seem so long?

ROMEO: The sadness that comes from love—

Or rather, from not having love.
The woman I love will not listen
To my sweet words, nor look into
My longing eyes, nor accept gifts of gold.
She is rich in beauty. It is so sad that her
Treasure of beauty will die with her.

BENVOLIO: Then she has sworn that she will
live chaste?

ROMEO: She has. And it seems such a waste
That her beauty won't be passed on
to any child.
She has sworn off love, and that cruel vow
Makes me feel like dying now.

BENVOLIO: Listen to me, cousin.
Forget to think of her!

ROMEO: Oh, teach me how to do that!

BENVOLIO: Give liberty to your eyes.
Look at other beauties.

ROMEO: If I did, I would only think of her.
He who goes blind cannot forget
The precious treasure of his lost eyesight.
Show me a woman who is beautiful,
And her beauty would only make me think
Of one who is even more beautiful.
Farewell. You cannot teach me to forget!

BENVOLIO: I will, or I'll die trying!

*(**Romeo** and **Benvolio** exit.)*

Scene 2

*(A street in Verona. **Lord Capulet, Paris,** and a **servant** enter.)*

CAPULET: Montague must obey the prince, too.
It shouldn't be too hard, I think,
For men as old as we are to keep the peace.

PARIS: You are both men of good reputation.
It's a pity you have been enemies for so long!
But now, my lord, what do you say about
My request to marry your daughter Juliet?

CAPULET: I say what I have said before.
My child is still a stranger in the world.
She is not yet 14 years old.
Let two more summers pass before
She will be ready to be a bride.

PARIS: Many girls younger than Juliet
Have become happy mothers.

CAPULET: Such girls are more often ruined.
All my other children have died.
Juliet is the only child I have left.
But woo her, gentle Paris. Get her heart.
My wishes are not as important as hers.
If she agrees, then I will consent.
Tonight I am giving a dinner party.
I have invited many guests.
You are invited, too.
Come to my humble home tonight.

You will see young beauties that,
Like stars, make the dark nighttime bright.
Hear all, see all. Maybe you will decide
That you would prefer a different bride.
(to the servant, giving him a piece of paper): Go
    through fair Verona. Find the persons
Listed here and tell them that I hope to
    see them at the party tonight.

*(**Paris** and **Capulet** exit.)*

SERVANT *(aside)*: *Find those named on this list!*
    He has forgotten that I cannot read.
    I must find someone who can.

*(**Benvolio** and **Romeo** enter.)*

BENVOLIO: I have some more advice for you.
    One fire can burn out another one.
    One pain stops when another one starts.
    One great grief is cured with a greater
        one. Fall in love with someone else,
    And the poison of your old love will die.

ROMEO: I am in a prison of my own sorrow.
    Nothing can help me, Benvolio.
    (to the servant): Good day, good fellow.

SERVANT: Good day to you. May I ask, sir, can
    you read?

ROMEO: Yes, I can read my own sad future.

SERVANT: Perhaps you can read that without a
    book. But can you read anything you see?

ROMEO: Yes, if it is in a language that I know.

SERVANT *(giving Romeo the list)*: Please read this.

ROMEO *(reading)*: "Martino and his wife and daughters, Count Anselmo and his beautiful sisters, the widow of Vitruvio, Placentio and his lovely nieces, Mercutio and his brother Valentine, my uncle Capulet and his wife and daughters, my fair niece Rosaline, Livia, Valentio and his cousin Tybalt, Lucio and the lively Helena." That's quite a group. *(He returns the list.)* Where should they come?

SERVANT: To supper at our house.

ROMEO: Whose house?

SERVANT: My master, the great rich Capulet. And if you are not of the house of Montague, you may come and have a drink, too. Goodbye now.

*(The **servant** exits.)*

BENVOLIO: Rosaline, whom you love so much,
Will be at Capulet's feast. Go there, Romeo.
Compare her face to others you will see.
I'll make you think your swan is but a crow.

ROMEO: A face more beautiful than Rosaline's?
If my eye believed such a lie,
Then tears would turn to fires!
One fairer than my love? The all-seeing sun
Has never seen her match!

14

BENVOLIO: How do you know, Romeo?
  You have never compared her to another.
  Tonight, look at some of the other girls.
  I'll show you that Rosaline is not
  The only girl in Verona.

ROMEO: I'll go—no such sight to be shown,
  But to enjoy the beauty of my own.

(*Romeo* and *Benvolio* exit.)

Scene 3

*(A room in Capulet's house. **Lady Capulet** and **Nurse** enter.)*

LADY CAPULET: Nurse, where's my daughter?
  Call her.

NURSE: Juliet!

(*Juliet* enters.)

JULIET: Who wants to see me?

NURSE: Your mother.

JULIET: Mother, I am here. What is your wish?

LADY CAPULET: Nurse, leave us now.
  We must talk in secret. No, wait, come back.
  You may stay and listen.
  You know my daughter's age.

NURSE: Of course. I can tell her age to the hour.

LADY CAPULET: She's not 14.

15

NURSE: I'll bet 14 of my teeth, though I have only four of them, that she will be 14 soon. In fact, she will be 14 in about two weeks. It's hard to believe. She was the most beautiful baby I have ever taken care of. I only hope I live long enough to see her get married.

LADY CAPULET: That is the very thing
I want to talk about.
(to Juliet): Tell me, daughter Juliet,
How do you feel about getting married?

JULIET: It is an honor that I do not dream about.

LADY CAPULET: Well, think of marriage now.
Many girls of Verona, younger than you,
Are already mothers. When I was your age,
I was already your mother. Did you know
That the worthy Paris seeks you for his love?

NURSE: What luck, Juliet! He's a fine man!

LADY CAPULET: Verona's summer does not have
such a flower!

NURSE: Yes, he's a flower, all right—a real flower!

LADY CAPULET: What do you say?
Can you love the gentleman?
Tonight you will see him at our dinner party.
Study his face. Read his eyes.
See him as a precious book of love
That lacks only a cover.
If you marry him, you shall share all he has,

16

And become better yourself.
Do you think you could love Paris?

JULIET: If looking leads to liking, I could.
But I will look only as much as I have to,
Because you have asked me to.

*(A **servant** enters.)*

SERVANT: Madam, the guests are here, and
your presence is requested.

LADY CAPULET: We will follow you.

*(**Servant** exits.)*

Juliet, Paris is waiting for you.

NURSE: Go, my girl. Happy days will lead to
happy nights!

*(**Lady Capulet, Juliet**, and **Nurse** exit.)*

Scene 4

*(A street in Verona. **Romeo, Mercutio**, and **Benvolio**
enter, with **five or six others**. The others are wearing
party masks.)*

ROMEO: How shall we present ourselves?
Should we just go in silently?

BENVOLIO: We don't have to say anything
As we go in. Let them take us as they will.
We'll have a dance, and then be gone.

ROMEO: Give me a torch to carry instead.
I don't feel like dancing.
Being in a dark mood, I will bear the light.

MERCUTIO: No, gentle Romeo. You must dance.

ROMEO: Not me. You have dancing shoes
With light soles. My soul is so heavy
I am stuck to the ground. I cannot move.

MERCUTIO: You are a lover—
Borrow Cupid's wings and fly!

ROMEO: I am too sore from Cupid's arrows
To fly with his light feathers.
I sink under love's heavy burden.

MERCUTIO: Sink? You use strange words
To describe such a tender thing as love.

ROMEO: Is love a tender thing? To me,
It is too rough, too rude, too difficult.
It cuts like a thorn.

MERCUTIO: If love is rough with you,
Be rough with love. Cut love for cutting you,
And you beat love down.
We're almost there. Give me my mask. *(He puts on a mask.)*

BENVOLIO: Here we are. Knock and enter.
As soon as we get in, start dancing.

ROMEO: Only a torch for me.
Let those who are light of heart
Tickle the floor with their heels.

I'll be a candle-holder and look on.

MERCUTIO: We'll get you out of this bad mood.
Come on.

ROMEO: We mean well, in going to this party,
But it is not a good idea to go.

MERCUTIO: Why, may one ask?

ROMEO: I dreamed a dream last night.

MERCUTIO: Ah! Queen Mab has been with you.
She is the Fairy Queen no bigger than a gem
On the ring on a man's finger. She travels
In a tiny carriage drawn by little creatures
Across men's noses as they lie asleep.
Her wagon-spokes are made of spiders' legs.
The cover is made of grasshoppers' wings.
The reins are of the smallest spider's web.
Her whip is made of cricket's bone.
Her driver is a small gray gnat,
Not half so big as a round little worm.
Her chariot is an empty hazel nut.
In this state, she gallops night after night
Through lovers' brains—they dream of love.
Over lawyers' fingers—they dream of fees.
Over ladies' lips—they dream of kisses.
This is the same Mab who tickles
A parson's nose as he lies asleep.
This is the same Mab that braids the manes
Of horses in the night
And tangles your hair in bed.

ROMEO: Enough, Mercutio, please!
   You talk about nothing.

MERCUTIO: True, I talk of dreams,
   Which are the children of an idle brain.
   They are nothing but fantasy,
   Thin as the air, more fickle than the wind.

BENVOLIO: This wind you talk of
   Has blown us the wrong way.
   Supper is done, and we shall come too late.

ROMEO: I fear we are too early. I have a feeling
   That something awful is hanging in the stars,
   And will begin its fearful trip at this party.
   I feel that it will lead to my early death.
   But may He who has so far steered my life
   Direct my sail! Press on, gentlemen!

BENVOLIO: Strike, drum.

*(They **all** exit.)*

Scene 5

*(A hall in Capulet's house. Musicians are waiting.
Servants enter.)*

FIRST SERVANT: Where is Potpan? He should be
   helping us clear away these plates.

SECOND SERVANT: When you depend on Potpan,
   you are always disappointed.

FIRST SERVANT: Take the stools away. Remove
the table, and look after the silver. Go
tell the porter to send in Susan
Grindstone and Nell.

*(**Second servant** exits. **Lord and Lady Capulet** enter,
along with **Juliet, Tybalt, Nurse, guests**, and **musicians**.)*

CAPULET: Welcome, gentlemen! The ladies
Whose toes are without corns
Will dance with you. Ah, ha, my ladies!
Which of you all will dance?
If you refuse, I'll swear you have corns!
Welcome, gentlemen: I remember the days
I wore a mask to a dance and told
A whispering tale in a fair lady's ear.
Those days are gone, are gone!
Come, musicians, play!

(Music plays, and they dance.)

More light! Move these tables!
And put out the fire—the room is too hot.
Ah, hello! Sit, good cousin Capulet,
For you and I are past our dancing days.
How long is it since we wore masks?

COUSIN CAPULET: Bless me—30 years!

CAPULET: What, man! It's not that long.
It's been 25 years since Lucentio's wedding.
We wore masks then.

COUSIN CAPULET: It's longer, it's longer.

21

His son is older than that, sir.
His son is 30.

CAPULET: But that's not possible.
His son was but a baby two years ago.

ROMEO *(to a servant)*: What lady is that
Who dances with that knight?

SERVANT: I do not know, sir.

ROMEO: She could teach torches to burn bright!
She hangs upon the cheek of night
Like a rich jewel in an Ethiopian's ear.
Her beauty is too rich for use—far too dear!
She is like a snow-white dove among crows.
She shines like stars, like candles she glows.
The song is over. I'll see where she stands.
Barely touching her will bless my hands.
Did my heart love until now? You lied to
    me, sight! For I never saw
True beauty before this night!

TYBALT: I know that voice! He is a Montague!
Fetch me my sword, boy. Does he dare
Come here, covered with a party mask,
To mock us at our own party?
By the honor of my kin,
I'll strike him dead and not call it a sin.

CAPULET: Tybalt! Why are you so angry?

TYBALT: Uncle, that man is a Montague.
The villain, our foe, has come here in spite
To mock us and spoil our party tonight.

CAPULET: Young Romeo, is it?

TYBALT: Yes, it is. That villain, Romeo.

CAPULET: Calm down, cousin. Let him be.
He looks like a well-behaved gentleman.
And, to tell the truth, all of Verona says
He is a decent and well-mannered youth.
Not for all the wealth of this town
Would I be rude to him here in my home.
So be patient. Take no note of him.
It is my wish. If you respect me,
Be polite and stop frowning.
It is no way to behave at a party.

TYBALT: It is, when such a villain is a guest.
I don't want him to stay.

CAPULET: You will tolerate him.
Am I in charge here, or are you?
You'll ruin the party if you keep this up.
You may either go away or be quiet.

TYBALT: I am so upset that I will leave.
But I won't forget about this.

(Tybalt exits.)

ROMEO *(to Juliet)***:** If my unworthy hand
Dishonors yours, it would be like
Dishonoring a holy shrine.
I would make up for it like this—
My lips would smooth that rough touch
With a tender kiss.

23

JULIET: Good sir, you talk too much
About the roughness of your hand.
Don't pilgrims pray by touching their
Hands palm to palm?

ROMEO: And do we not also pray with our lips?
So then, dear lady, let lips do what hands do!
(They kiss.)

NURSE: Your mother would like to see you.

(Juliet exits.)

ROMEO: Who is her mother?

NURSE: The lady of the house, wise and
virtuous.
I tell you, he who marries her
Shall be rich.

ROMEO *(to Benvolio)***:** Is she a Capulet?
Oh, no! My life is in my foe's hands.

BENVOLIO: Let's go, Romeo. The party is over.

ROMEO: Yes, so I fear, much to my sorrow.

CAPULET: No, gentlemen, don't go yet.
We have some more refreshments.
Must you leave? Well, thank you for coming.
*(to the servants)***:** More lights here!
*(to Lady Capulet)***:** Come. Let's go to bed.

(All exit but Juliet and Nurse.)

JULIET: Come here, Nurse. Who is the
Young man who would not dance?

NURSE: I do not know.

JULIET: Go and find out his name.

*(**Nurse** leaves.)*

If he is married, the only wedding bed
I'll have will be my grave!

*(**Nurse** returns.)*

NURSE: His name is Romeo. He's a Montague,
The only son of your family's great enemy.

JULIET: My only love comes from my only hate!
If I had only known! Now it is too late!
How could this have happened to me?
Why must I love my family's enemy?

NURSE: What's all this? What's all this?

JULIET: It's just a rhyme I learned tonight.

(A voice from another room calls, "Juliet.")

NURSE: Come! Come! Let's go to bed.
The guests are all gone.

*(**Juliet** and **Nurse** exit.)*

ACT 2

Scene 1

*(An open place just outside the wall of Capulet's garden. **Romeo** enters.)*

ROMEO: How can I go when my heart is here?
I must stay and find my center.
(He climbs the wall and leaps over it.)

*(**Benvolio** and **Mercutio** enter.)*

BENVOLIO: Romeo! My cousin, Romeo!

MERCUTIO: If he is wise, he's gone home to bed.

BENVOLIO: No, I think he ran this way
And leaped over the orchard wall.
Call out, good Mercutio.

MERCUTIO: I'll call him with magic words.
Romeo! Madman! Passionate lover!
Appear to us in the likeness of a sigh.
Speak just one rhyme, and I'll be happy.
Say, "Ah, me!" Or say "love" and "dove."
Speak to Venus, the goddess of love.
Say a few words for her son Cupid.
(Mercutio listens, but Romeo does not answer.)

MERCUTIO: He hears nothing. I will use magic
To bring him back. What shall I say?
Ah, I know: By Rosaline's bright eyes,

By her high forehead and her red lips,
By her fine feet and straight legs,
I summon you to appear to us!

BENVOLIO *(laughing)*: If he hears you, you will
  anger him.

MERCUTIO: This cannot anger him.
  My spell is fair and honest.
  I used Rosaline's name to get his attention.

BENVOLIO: He has hid himself among these trees,
  So he can be alone with the night.
  His blind love sees best in the dark.

MERCUTIO: If love is blind, it cannot hit the mark.
  He might be sitting under a fruit tree,
  Wishing his love were that kind of fruit.
  (calling to Romeo): Romeo, good night.
  It's too cold in this field for me to sleep.
  Come, shall we go?

BENVOLIO: Let's go, then.
  It is foolish to seek him here.
  He doesn't want to be found.

(Benvolio and **Mercutio** exit.)

Scene 2

(Capulet's orchard. **Romeo** *enters.)*

ROMEO: Mercutio laughs at love's scars,
  But he has never felt a wound.

27

*(**Juliet** appears above at a window.)*

But, oh, what light comes through that
  window?
It is the east, and Juliet is the sun!
Arise, fair sun, and kill the jealous moon,
Who is already sick and pale with grief
Because you are far more fair than she.
It is my lady. Oh, it is my love!
Oh, if only she knew how I feel!
She speaks, yet she says nothing.
Her eye speaks, but not to me.
Two of the fairest stars in all the heaven
Have business elsewhere. They ask her eyes
To twinkle until they return.
What if her eyes were in the heavens,
And the stars were in her head?
The brightness of her cheek would shame
  those stars,
As daylight shames a lamp. Her eyes in
  heaven
Would make the sky so bright
That birds would sing, thinking it was not
  night.
See how she leans her cheek upon her hand!
If only I were a glove upon that hand
That I might touch her cheek!

JULIET: Oh, my!

ROMEO: She speaks.

Oh, speak again, bright angel! For you are
As glorious as a winged angel of heaven.

JULIET: Oh, Romeo, Romeo! Why are you a
Montague?
Deny your father and refuse your name.
Or, if you will not, swear to be my love,
And I'll no longer be a Capulet.

ROMEO *(aside)***:** Shall I listen to more,
Or shall I dare to speak?

JULIET: Only your name is my enemy.
What's a Montague? It is not hand, nor foot,
Nor arm, nor face, nor any other part
Belonging to a man. Oh, take some other
name!

29

What's in a name? A rose
By any other name would smell as sweet.
So Romeo would still be perfect,
If he were not called Montague.
Romeo, take off your name.
And for that name, which is no part of you,
Take all of me.

ROMEO: I take you at your word.
Call me your love, and I'll have a new name.
From now on, I will never be Romeo.

JULIET: Who are you, hidden in the night,
Listening to what I say?

ROMEO: I don't know how to tell you who I am.
My name, dear lady, is hateful to me
Because it is an enemy to you.
If it were written, I would tear the paper.

JULIET: My ears have heard less than 100 words
From that mouth—yet I know the sound.
Are you not Romeo, and a Montague?

ROMEO: Neither, fair lady, if you dislike either.

JULIET: How did you get here? Tell me!
The orchard walls are high and hard to climb.
And this place could mean your death,
Considering who you are,
If any of my kinsmen find you here.

ROMEO: I flew over these walls with love's
light wings.

Stone walls cannot hold back love.
And what love can do, love dares to try.
So your kinsmen cannot stop me.

JULIET: If they see you, they will murder you.

ROMEO: There is more danger in your eye
Than in 20 of their swords. Just look sweet,
And I am ready to fight their hatred.

JULIET: I would not, for the world, want them
to see you here.

ROMEO: I have night's cloak to hide me.
And, if you don't love me, let them find me.
It would be better to end my life by their
hate than to live without your love.

JULIET: Who told you how to find this place?

ROMEO: Love told me. I am not a ship's pilot.
But if you were a far shore washed with
The farthest sea, I would sail to find you.

JULIET: The mask of night is on my face.
Otherwise, you would see me blush
For what you have heard me say tonight.
Do you love me? I know you will say yes.
And I will take your word.
But do not swear it, for you may be lying.
When lovers lie, they say the gods laugh.
Oh, gentle Romeo, say it faithfully.
Or, if you think I am too quickly won,
I'll frown so you will charm me more.

But the truth is, fair Montague,
I am too fond of you to pretend.
You may think I am not modest,
But trust me, gentleman, I'll be more true
Than those who are more cunning.
I should have been more coy, perhaps,
But you overheard my true feelings,
Before I was aware that you were here.
My true love, please forgive me.
My love is not as light as it might seem.

ROMEO: Lady, I swear by the moon that—

JULIET: Oh, do not swear by the moon.
It changes from one night to the next.

ROMEO: What shall I swear by?

JULIET: Do not swear at all.
Or, if you must, swear by your gracious self,
Which is the god I adore,
And I'll believe you.

ROMEO: By my heart's dear love—

JULIET: No, do not swear.
Although you give me joy,
I have no joy about our love tonight.
It is too rash, too fast, too sudden.
Too much like lightning, which is gone
Before you can even say,
"Look, lightning!" Good night!
This bud of our love may bloom into a

Beautiful flower when we meet again.
Good night, good night! May sweet rest
Come to your heart as it has come to mine!

ROMEO: Oh, will you leave me so unsatisfied?

JULIET: What satisfaction can you have tonight?

ROMEO: I wish you to exchange your faithful
   vow of love for mine.

JULIET: I gave you mine before you asked for it.
   And yet I would take it back.

ROMEO: You would take it back? Why, love?

JULIET: So I could give it to you again.
   My love is as deep as the sea.
   The more I give to you, the more I have,
   For both are endless.

(Nurse calls from offstage.)

   I hear some noise inside. Dear love, farewell!

(Nurse calls again.)

   Just a moment, good nurse!
   Sweet Montague, be true.
   Wait here a moment, I will come out again.

*(**Juliet** exits.)*

ROMEO: Oh, blessed, blessed night. I fear,
   Since it is night, that this is just a dream,
   Too sweet to be real.

*(**Juliet** enters again, above.)*

JULIET: Three words, dear Romeo,
   And then good night. If your love
   Is honorable and you want to wed,
   Send me word tomorrow.
   I'll send someone to get your message.
   Tell me where and when we will marry.
   Then I'll lay all my fortunes at your feet
   And follow you throughout the world.

NURSE *(from offstage)*: Madam!

JULIET: I'm coming!
   (to Romeo): But if you do not want to
      marry me,
   I beg you to leave me alone to my grief.
   A thousand times good night!

*(**Juliet** exits.)*

ROMEO: It is a thousand times worse,
   Now that she is gone.

*(**Juliet** enters again, above.)*

JULIET: Romeo!

ROMEO: It is my soul that calls my name.
   What a silver-sweet sound!
   It is like softest music to attentive ears!

JULIET: Romeo!

ROMEO: My dear?

JULIET: At what time tomorrow
   Shall I send a messenger to you?

ROMEO: At the hour of nine.

JULIET: I will not fail.
It will seem like 20 years until then.
Good night, good night!
Parting is such sweet sorrow
That I could say good night until tomorrow.

*(**Juliet** exits.)*

ROMEO: Sleep well, and peace be in your heart!
I will visit Friar Lawrence in his monk's cell,
His help to ask and my good fortune to tell.

*(**Romeo** exits.)*

Scene 3

*(**Friar Lawrence** enters his cell, carrying a basket.)*

FRIAR: Morning smiles on frowning night,
Filling eastern clouds with streaks of light.
Before the sun dries up the morning dew,
I must fill this basket with plants.
The earth, which is nature's mother,
Is also her grave. Her greenery
Can both help us and harm us.
Great power lies in herbs, plants, and
    stones.
Nothing that lives on the earth is so foul
That it doesn't have some good in it. And
Nothing is so good that it cannot be abused.
Virtue itself can become vice, if misused.

This small flower holds poison and medicine.
Smelling it will help any sick part,
But tasting it will kill the strongest heart.
In people and in plants, good and evil lie.

(Romeo enters.)

ROMEO: Good morning, Father!

FRIAR: Bless you!
Who salutes me so sweetly this early?
Son, it suggests a troubled head
To rise so early and leave your bed.
Worry often keeps old men awake,
But young men with no worries sleep well.
Therefore, your early rising makes me think
That some trouble has kept you awake.
Tell me if I am right.
Or is it that you did not go to bed last night?

ROMEO: What you said last is true.

FRIAR: My goodness! Were you with Rosaline?

ROMEO: With Rosaline, Father? No.
I have forgotten that name, and its woe.

FRIAR: Good, my son. But where have you been?

ROMEO: I'll tell you before you ask me again.
I went to a party given by our enemy.
There I was wounded by one of them,
That I also wounded. We can be cured
With your help. I feel no hatred, Father,
And neither does my foe.

FRIAR: Be plain, my son.
   You are speaking in riddles,
   And I don't understand you.

ROMEO: Here is the plain truth.
   My heart's dear love is set
   On the fair daughter of rich Capulet.
   As I love her, so she also loves me.
   We want to be married! I'll tell you later
   The story of when, where, and how we met,
   And wooed, and made exchange of vow.
   But for now, I ask—indeed, I pray—
   That you agree to marry us today.

FRIAR: Holy Saint Francis! What a change!
   Is Rosaline, whom you did love so dear,
   So soon forgotten?
   Young men's love, then, lies
   Not truly in their hearts, but in their eyes.
   How many tears washed your cheeks
   For Rosaline! How much salt water
   Thrown away in waste,
   To season love, that you never taste!
   The sun has not yet cleared your sighs away.
   Your old groans still ring in my old ears.
   Look, here on your cheek is the stain
   Of an old tear that is not washed off yet.
   How are you so changed?

ROMEO: You often scolded me for loving Rosaline.
   You told me to bury my love.

FRIAR: But you have buried one, and dug up
  another.

ROMEO: Please don't scold me, Father!
  The one I love now returns my love.
  The other did not.

FRIAR: Come now and go with me.
  Your assistant in this I'll gladly be.
  This marriage may prove in the end,
  To turn your families into friends.

ROMEO: Let us go! I want this done quickly.

FRIAR: Be wise, my son, careful and slow.
  You'll stumble if you too fast go.

(Romeo and Friar Lawrence exit.)

Scene 4

*(A street. **Benvolio** and **Mercutio** enter.)*

MERCUTIO: Where the devil could Romeo be?
  Didn't he come home last night?

BENVOLIO: Not to his father's house, I hear.

MERCUTIO: Ah, that cold-hearted Rosaline
  Torments him so that he will surely go mad.

BENVOLIO: Tybalt, a Capulet cousin,
  Has sent a letter to Romeo's house.

MERCUTIO: I'll bet it's a challenge to a duel.

BENVOLIO: Romeo will answer it.

MERCUTIO: So? Any man who can write may
    answer a letter.

BENVOLIO: I mean, Romeo will answer by
    accepting the dare.

MERCUTIO: Poor Romeo. He is already dead!
    Stabbed in the eye with Rosaline's looks,
    Shot through the ear with a love song,
    Pierced in the heart with Cupid's arrow.
    Is he strong enough to meet Tybalt?

BENVOLIO: Why, what is Tybalt?

MERCUTIO: A bigger threat than you know.
    He is an expert with the sword.
    His timing, pace, and rhythm are perfect.
    He has gone to the best fencing schools
    And sliced many a button off a silk shirt.

(Romeo enters.)

BENVOLIO: Here comes Romeo!

MERCUTIO: Good morning, Romeo!
    You got away from us last night.

ROMEO: Good morning to you both.
    I'm sorry for last night.
    I had some important business to see to.
    But it's all taken care of now.

MERCUTIO: Who's that coming up the street?

*(Juliet's **Nurse** enters.)*

NURSE: Good morning, gentlemen.

MERCUTIO: Good morning, fair gentlewoman.

NURSE: Can any of you tell me where I may find the young Romeo?

ROMEO: I can tell you. But young Romeo is getting older even as you are looking at him. For better or worse, I am Romeo.

NURSE: Then I need to talk with you privately.

ROMEO *(to Benvolio and Mercutio)***:** My friends,
You go on to my father's.
I'll meet you there later.

(*Mercutio* and *Benvolio* exit.)

NURSE: My lady Juliet asked me to find you. Before I give you her message, first let me tell you something. She is a young and good woman. You had better not be toying with her or leading her on. If you are lying to her, you will have to deal with me!

ROMEO: Nurse, send my greetings to your lady.
I promise you—

NURSE: Bless your heart! I can see that you are sincere. She will be glad to hear your greetings.

ROMEO: Tell her to meet me this afternoon
At Friar Lawrence's cell.
There we will be married.

NURSE: This afternoon, sir? She'll be there.

ROMEO: One more thing, good nurse.
Wait behind that wall over there.
My servant will meet you within the hour.
He will bring a rope ladder.
Hide it in the orchard, near Juliet's window.
Tonight I will use it to climb up to her room.
Keep our secret, and I'll reward you.

NURSE: Bless you, sir. But listen,
Can your servant keep a secret?
Have you ever heard the saying,
"Two may keep a secret, if one is dead"?

ROMEO: My servant is as true as steel.

NURSE: Well, sir, my lady is very sweet. There's a count in town, named Paris. He wants to marry Juliet himself. But she would rather see a toad than see him. When I tell her that Paris is a better man than you, she turns pale.

ROMEO: My regards to your lady.

NURSE: Yes, a thousand times.

*(**Romeo** and **Nurse** exit.)*

Scene 5

*(Capulet's orchard. **Juliet** enters.)*

JULIET: It was nine when the nurse left.
She said she'd return in half an hour.

41

Maybe she did not meet him. She is so slow!
  Love's messengers should be thoughts,
Which glide faster than the sun's beams
As they drive back shadows over the hills.
Now the sun has crossed the highest hill
Of this day's journey. From nine to twelve is
Three long hours, yet she is still not here.
If she felt love and had warm, youthful
  blood,
She'd be as swift as a rolling ball.
My words would hurry her to my sweet love,
And his words to me.
But old folks act as if they were dead,
Clumsy, slow, heavy, and pale as lead.
Oh, God! Here she comes!

(Nurse enters.)

Oh, sweet nurse, what news do you have?
Have you met with him?

NURSE: I am tired. Let me rest a while.
How my bones ache! What a trip I've had!

JULIET: I wish you had my bones, and I had
your news!
Now, I beg you, good nurse, speak.

NURSE: Can't you wait a minute? Do you not
see that I am out of breath?

JULIET: How can you be out of breath, when you
Have breath to tell me you are out of breath?
Your excuses take longer than the news!

Is the news good or bad?
What does he say about our marriage?

NURSE: Lord, how my head aches!
It feels as if it would break in 20 pieces.
Oh, my back, my back! Shame on you
For sending me all over town.

JULIET: I am sorry that you are not feeling well.
Sweet nurse, tell me what my love said.

NURSE: Your love says, like a kind gentleman,
And courteous, handsome, and virtuous—
But where is your mother?

JULIET: Where is my mother? Why, she is inside.
What does he want with my mother?

NURSE: Oh, dear! You are angry. Is this how
You give comfort for my aching bones?
From now on, do your messages yourself.

JULIET: You're making such a fuss!
Come, tell me. What did Romeo say?

NURSE: Do you have permission to
Go to confession today?

JULIET: I have.

NURSE: Then go to Friar Lawrence's cell.
There waits a husband to make you a wife.
I see that you are blushing!
Get to church. I must go another way
To get a ladder, which Romeo will use
To climb to your room when it is dark.

43

I am the drudge, and work for your delight.
But you'll be on your own tonight.
Now, go to the friar's cell.

JULIET: I'm on my way! Dear nurse, farewell.

*(**Nurse** and **Juliet** exit.)*

Scene 6

*(**Friar Lawrence** and **Romeo** enter the friar's cell.)*

FRIAR: May the heavens smile on this holy act.
May it not cause any sorrow in the future.

ROMEO: Amen! But whatever sorrow comes,
It cannot take away the joy
That one minute gives me in her sight.
If you but join our hands with holy words,
Then love-eating death may do what he dare.
It is enough that I may just call her mine.

FRIAR: These violent delights have violent ends,
And die too soon, like fire and gunpowder,
When they kiss and destroy each other.
The sweetest honey can be sickening.
So love moderately. It will last longer.

*(**Juliet** enters. Romeo kisses her.)*

Here is the lady. When I see
Her light walk, I think their love will last.
A lover may ride a spider's web

That drifts in the lazy summer air,
And does not fall. The joys in life are
  that light.

ROMEO: Juliet, if your joy is as great as mine,
And you can describe it, then sweeten the air
With your words. Let them express the
Great happiness we feel
Because of this dear meeting.

JULIET: My joy is richer than words can say.
Only beggars can really count their worth.
But my true love has grown to such excess,
I cannot count up half my wealth.

FRIAR: Come with me. We will do this quickly.
For—begging your pardons—
You two cannot stay alone
Until the church has made you one.

*(**Romeo, Juliet**, and **Friar Lawrence** exit.)*

ACT 3 Scene 1

*(**Mercutio, Benvolio**, and **servants** enter a public place.)*

BENVOLIO: Mercutio, let's go home.
The day is hot, and the Capulets are out.
If we meet, there will be a fight.
These hot days get the mad blood stirring.

MERCUTIO: You are like one of those fellows who slaps down his sword on a tavern table and says, "I hope I won't be needing you!" By the time he's had his second drink, he's drawn his sword against the bartender, for no good reason.

BENVOLIO: Am I like such a fellow?

MERCUTIO: Come, come! You are as hot-blooded as anyone in Italy, and as quick to get angry! If there were two of you, we should soon have none—for one would kill the other. Why, you would quarrel with a man for having a hair more or less in his beard than you have. You would quarrel with a man for cracking nuts, having no other reason but that you have hazel eyes. Who but you would quarrel over that? Your head is as full of quarrels as an egg is full of meat. And yet your head has been beaten like an egg for quarreling. You have quarreled with a man for coughing in the street because he woke up your dog. You quarreled with a tailor for wearing his new coat before Easter. And yet you tell *me* not to quarrel!

BENVOLIO: Ha! If I quarreled as much as you, my life would not last another hour!

MERCUTIO: You said it, not I!

BENVOLIO: By my head, here come the Capulets.

MERCUTIO: By my heel, I do not care.

(Tybalt and others enter.)

TYBALT *(to his friends)*: Stay close, for I will speak to them.
  (to Benvolio and Mercutio): Gentlemen, good day. A word with one of you?

MERCUTIO: Just a word? How about a word and a fight?

TYBALT: You shall find me ready for that, sir, if you give me a reason.

MERCUTIO: Can't you find a reason without my giving you one?

TYBALT: Mercutio, you are one of Romeo's band—

MERCUTIO: Band! What do you think we are,
   musicians? *(waving his sword)***:** Here's my
   fiddlestick! That shall make you dance!

BENVOLIO: We are in a public place.
   Either go into some private place
   To talk about your differences,
   Or else leave. Here all eyes gaze on us.

MERCUTIO: Men's eyes were made to gaze.
   I will not budge to please anyone.

TYBALT: Well, peace be with you, sir.

*(**Romeo** enters.)*

   Here comes the man I'm looking for.
      Romeo, you are a villain!

ROMEO: Tybalt, I have my reasons for excusing
   your insult.
   I am not a villain. Therefore, farewell.
   I see that you don't really know me.

TYBALT: Boy, this does not excuse the injuries
   You have done me. So, turn and draw.

ROMEO: I never injured you.
   I love you more than you can dream—
   Until you know the reason for my love.
   And so, good Capulet, which name I love
   As dearly as my own, calm down.

MERCUTIO: What are you saying, Romeo? *(He
   draws his sword.)* Tybalt, you rat-catcher,
   will you walk away?

TYBALT: What do you want with me?

MERCUTIO: Good king of cats, nothing but one of your nine lives!

TYBALT *(drawing his sword)***:** I am ready for you!

ROMEO: Gentle Mercutio, put your sword away.

MERCUTIO: Come, sir, your move.

ROMEO: Stop! Remember what the Prince said about fighting on the streets of Verona! Stop, Tybalt! Please, good Mercutio!

(As Mercutio and Tybalt fight, Romeo steps between them. Tybalt, shielded by Romeo, thrusts his sword into Mercutio's body. Then Tybalt runs away with his friends.)

MERCUTIO: I am hurt. I am dying!
　A plague on both your houses!
　Is he gone, and has no injuries?

BENVOLIO: What, are you hurt?

MERCUTIO: Yes, yes. A scratch, a scratch.
　But it is enough. Where is my servant?
　Go, get a doctor.

*(**Servant** exits.)*

ROMEO: Courage, man. The hurt can't be much.

MERCUTIO: No, it is not as deep as a well, nor
　as wide as a church door. But it is
　enough, it will serve. Ask for me
　tomorrow, and you shall find me a grave
　man. I am not long for this world. A
　plague on both your houses! Only a dog,
　a rat, a mouse, a cat scratches a man to
　death! Why did you come between us?
　He struck me by going under your arm.

ROMEO: I thought I was doing the best thing.

MERCUTIO: Help me into some house,
　Benvolio, or I shall faint.
　A plague on both your houses!
　They have made worms' meat of me.

*(**Mercutio** and **Benvolio** exit.)*

ROMEO: This gentleman, my dear friend, has
　Been wounded because Tybalt insulted me.

Tybalt—my relative for the past hour!
Oh, Juliet, your beauty has made me weak!

*(**Benvolio** enters again.)*

BENVOLIO: Oh, Romeo, Romeo,
Brave Mercutio's dead!

ROMEO: This black day is, I fear,
Just the beginning. More woes will follow.

BENVOLIO: The furious Tybalt is back again.

ROMEO: Tybalt is alive, and Mercutio is dead!

*(**Tybalt** enters.)*

Now, Tybalt, you are the villain!
Mercutio's soul is just above our heads,
Waiting for yours to keep him company.
Either you or I, or both, must go with him.

(They fight. Tybalt falls dead.)

BENVOLIO: Romeo, you must get away!
People are coming, and Tybalt is dead.
Don't just stand there.
The Prince will have you put to death
If you are caught. Run!

ROMEO: Oh, I am fortune's fool!

BENVOLIO: Why do you stay?

*(**Romeo** runs. The **Prince** enters, followed by **Lord and Lady Montague**, **Lord and Lady Capulet**, their **servants**, and **other citizens**.)*

PRINCE: Who started this fight? Where did
they go?

BENVOLIO: Oh, noble Prince, I can tell you
who was in this fatal fight.
The man who lies there killed Mercutio.
He was then killed by Romeo.

LADY CAPULET: Tybalt, my cousin! Oh, my
brother's child!
Oh, husband! Capulet blood has been
shed.
The Montagues must pay in kind.

PRINCE: Benvolio, what happened here?

BENVOLIO: Tybalt started it all by picking a fight.
Romeo tried to calm him down,
Reminding him of your wishes.
But Tybalt was deaf to words of peace.
Mercutio tried to defend Romeo but was
killed.
Romeo, in anger, then fought with Tybalt.
When Tybalt fell, Romeo did turn and fly.
This is the truth, or let Benvolio die.

LADY CAPULET: He is related to Romeo.
So he is lying to save Romeo's life.
I beg for justice, which you, Prince, must give.
Romeo killed Tybalt; Romeo must not live.

PRINCE: Romeo killed Tybalt, but Tybalt killed
Mercutio.
Who owes the price of Mercutio's life?

MONTAGUE: Not Romeo, Prince.
  He was Mercutio's friend.
  Tybalt got what he deserved.
  Romeo only ended what the law would
    have ended—Tybalt's life.

PRINCE: Romeo should not have taken the law
    into his own hands.
  For that, we send him into exile.
  I have my own interest in this fight.
  Mercutio was one of my relatives.
  I will impose so big a fine
  That you shall all feel this loss of mine.
  No more excuses, by all my power!
  If Romeo is found here, it's his last hour!
  Carry this body away, and listen to our will:
  Mercy is like murder, when it pardons
    those who kill.

(**All** exit.)

Scene 2

(**Juliet** enters a room in the Capulet house.)

JULIET: Hurry, Sun! Race to the west
  And bring in cloudy night
  To spread its dark curtain.
  Let Romeo leap to these arms, unseen.
  Lovers use the light of their own beauty.

53

Or, if love is blind, it best agrees with night.
Gentle night, cover my blushing cheeks
With your black mantle. Come, night.
Come, Romeo. Come, you day in night!
For you will lie upon the wings of night
Whiter than new snow on a raven's back.
Come, loving dark night, and
Give me my Romeo. When he shall die,
Take him and cut him out in little stars.
He will make the face of heaven so fine
That all the world will be in love with night,
And pay no worship to the bright sun.
Oh, I have bought the mansion of a love,
But not lived in it. I am like
An impatient child with new clothes,
Waiting for the party, so I can wear them.
Here comes my nurse, and she brings news.

*(**Nurse** enters, with the rope ladder.)*

NURSE: Here is the rope ladder Romeo
wanted. *(She throws it down.)*

JULIET: Oh, my! What's the news? Why are
you wringing your hands?

NURSE: He's dead, he's dead, he's dead!
We are finished, lady, we are finished!
Pity the day! He's gone, he's killed, he's dead!

JULIET: Can heaven be so envious of us?

NURSE: Romeo can, though heaven cannot.

Oh, Romeo, Romeo!
Who ever would have thought it? Romeo!

JULIET: Why are you tormenting me this way?
Has Romeo killed himself?

NURSE: I saw the wound with my own eyes.
A terrible sight! A pitiful corpse.
Pale, pale as ashes, all covered in blood.
I fainted at the sight.

JULIET: Oh, break, my heart! Break at once!
To prison, eyes! Never look on liberty!

NURSE: Oh, Tybalt, Tybalt, the best friend I had!
Oh, dear Tybalt! Honest gentleman!
That I should live to see you dead!

JULIET: What are you saying?
Are both Romeo and Tybalt dead?
My dear cousin, and my dearer husband?
Let the trumpets sound the general doom,
For who can live, if those two are gone?

NURSE: Tybalt is gone, and Romeo must leave.
Romeo, who killed him, has been banished.

JULIET: Oh, God! Did Romeo's hand shed
Tybalt's blood?

NURSE: It did, it did. Curse the day, it did!

JULIET: A snake's heart, hid by a flowery face!
Did any dragon ever keep so fair a cave?
Evil angel! Wolf-eating lamb! Oh, Romeo,
You are the opposite of what you seemed.

Oh, that such evil should live
In such a gorgeous palace!

NURSE: There's no faith, no truth, no honesty
In men. All of them are liars.
These griefs, these woes, these sorrows
Make me old. May shame come to Romeo!

JULIET: May your tongue be blistered for making
Such a wish! He was not born to shame.
Shame is ashamed to sit upon his brow,
For it is a throne where honor may sit.
Oh, what a beast I was to speak ill of him!

NURSE: You speak well of your cousin's killer?

JULIET: Shall I speak ill of my husband?
My lord, what words can clear your name,
When I, your own wife, have ruined it?
But why, villain, did you kill my cousin?
That villain cousin would have killed you.
Back, foolish tears, back to your well!
My husband lives, whom Tybalt would
  have killed.
And Tybalt is dead, who would have killed
  my husband.
All this is comfort. Why, then, do I weep?
Tybalt's death was sad enough, if it had
  ended there.
But Romeo is banished!
There is no end in that word's death.
Where are my father and mother, nurse?

NURSE: Weeping and wailing over Tybalt.
Shall you go to see them? I will take you
there.

JULIET: Are they washing his wounds with tears?
When their tears are dry,
Mine will still be falling for Romeo.
I will go to my wedding bed now.
Death, not Romeo, will be my husband.

NURSE: Go to your room. I will find Romeo
To comfort you. I know where he is.
Listen, your Romeo will be here tonight.
He is hiding in Friar Lawrence's cell.

JULIET: Oh, find him! Give him this ring
And tell him to come to say his last farewell.

*(**Both** exit.)*

Scene 3

*(**Friar Lawrence** enters his cell.)*

FRIAR: Romeo, come here, you fearful man.
Suffering loves you. You are married to trouble.

*(**Romeo** enters.)*

ROMEO: Father, what is the news?
What is the Prince's punishment?

FRIAR: You, my son, have too much bad luck.
The Prince has decided you will not die,
But you will be banished.

ROMEO: Banished? Be merciful—say death.
Banishment is worse than death to me.

FRIAR: You are banished from Verona.
Be patient, for the world is broad and wide.

ROMEO: There is no world outside Verona.
Everything I love is here.

FRIAR: You should be grateful to the Prince.
The lawful punishment is death,
But the kind prince, taking your side,
Has brushed aside the law, and
Spared your life. You should thank him.
This is an act of dear mercy,
And you don't see it.

ROMEO: It is torture, not mercy! Heaven is here,
Where Juliet lives. Every cat, and dog,
And little mouse lives here in heaven,
And may look at her—but Romeo may not.
Even flies are better off than Romeo. They
May look on the beauty of dear Juliet's hand,
And steal a kiss from her lips.
But Romeo may not. He is banished.
Flies may do it, but I must fly from here.
And yet you say that exile is not death!
Don't you have poison, a sharp knife,
Some sudden means of death—
Other than banishment—to kill me?

FRIAR: You foolish man. I'll give you some
Philosophy to comfort you.

ROMEO: Philosophy! Unless it can make a Juliet
    Replace a town, change a prince's sentence,
    It does not help me. Talk no more.

FRIAR: Oh, then I see that madmen have no ears.

ROMEO: Why should they, when wise men
    have no eyes?

FRIAR: Listen to me, Romeo!

ROMEO: Don't speak of what you do not feel.
    If you were as young as I and loved Juliet,
    Married an hour, and banished
    For killing her cousin, then you might speak.
    Then you might tear your hair as I do,
    And fall on the ground, as if to measure
    your own grave.

(A knocking is heard from offstage.)

FRIAR: Hide, Romeo! Someone is knocking.

ROMEO: No, I won't hide.

(More knocking.)

FRIAR: Listen! How they knock! Who's there?
    Romeo, get up, or you will be taken away.
    Stand up. Run to my study.
    Who knocks so hard? What do you want?

NURSE *(from offstage)***:** Let me in. I come from
    Lady Juliet.

FRIAR *(opening the door)***:** Welcome, then.

*(**Nurse** enters.)*

NURSE: Oh, tell me, Father, where is Romeo?

FRIAR: On the ground, drunk on his own tears.

NURSE: Oh, he is acting just like Juliet!
Blubbering and weeping, weeping and
blubbering.
Stand up. Be a man, for Juliet's sake.

ROMEO *(rising from the floor)*: Nurse!
Were you speaking of Juliet? How is she?
Does she think I am a murderer?
That I have stained the start of our joy
With blood so close to her own?
Where is she? And how is she, and
What does she say about our love?

NURSE: She says nothing, sir, but weeps and weeps.
She falls on her bed, and then gets up,
And calls Tybalt's name, cries for Romeo,
And then falls down again.

ROMEO: As if that name has murdered her,
Just as my hand murdered her cousin.
Father, where in my body does my name lie?
Tell me, so I may cut it out!

FRIAR: Calm down! Are you a man?
Your form says you are, but your tears
Are womanish. Your wild acts suggest
The angry fury of a beast! You surprise me.
Will you kill yourself? If you do, you will
Kill your wife, too, for you are one now.
Get hold of yourself, man!

Your Juliet is alive. You are blessed.
Tybalt would have killed you,
But you killed Tybalt. Be happy about that.
The law, which might have killed you,
Became your friend and exiled you instead.
You are fortunate.
A pack of blessings lies on your back.
Go, get to your love, as you planned.
Climb to her room and comfort her.
Leave before morning and go to Mantua.
Live there until we can find the right time
To announce your marriage. Then we can
Beg pardon of the Prince and call you back
With a hundred thousand times more joy
Than the sorrow in which you left.
Go now, Nurse. Remember me to your lady,
And tell her to hurry her family off to bed.
Their heavy sorrow should make that easy.
Romeo is coming.

NURSE: I'll tell my lady the news.

(Nurse exits.)

ROMEO: I feel better now, with this new plan!

FRIAR: Go now. Good night!
And remember to leave before dawn.
Wait in Mantua. From time to time,
I'll send your servant to you with news.
Give me your hand. Farewell. Good night.

ROMEO: If not for the joy that calls to me,

61

I would be sad to leave your company.
Farewell.

*(**Friar Lawrence** and **Romeo** exit.)*

Scene 4

*(**Lord and Lady Capulet** enter a room in their house with **Paris**.)*

CAPULET: We have not had time to talk to Juliet
About your wish to marry her.
She loved her cousin Tybalt dearly,
And so did I. Well, we were all born to die.
It's very late. She won't come down tonight.
But for your company,
I would have been in bed an hour ago.

PARIS: Times of woe are not good times to woo.
Madam, good night. Remember me to Juliet.

LADY CAPULET: I will talk to her tomorrow.
Tonight, she is shut up with her sorrow.

CAPULET: I think it might be a good idea
If you married Juliet soon. In this matter,
I think she will do as I think best.
Wife, go to her before you go to bed.
Talk to her of Paris's love.
And tell her, on Wednesday—
But wait, what day is this?

PARIS: Monday, my lord.

CAPULET: Monday! Ha, ha! Well, Wednesday is
  too soon.
  Let it be Thursday.
  (to his wife): Tell her she shall be married
  To this noble earl on Thursday.
  (to Paris): Will you be ready?
  We'll have a small wedding—a friend or two.
  It wouldn't be right to have a big party,
  So soon after Tybalt's untimely death.
  We'll have some half a dozen friends,
  And that's all. What do you say to Thursday?

PARIS: I wish Thursday were tomorrow.

CAPULET: Well, Thursday it will be, then.
  (to his wife): Go to Juliet before going to bed.
  Prepare her, wife, for her wedding day.
  (to Paris): Farewell, my lord. It is so late,
  That we may call it early by and by.
  Good night.

*(They **all** exit.)*

Scene 5

(Romeo and Juliet stand on the balcony, overlooking Capulet's garden.)

JULIET: Will you leave? It is not yet day.
  It was the nightingale, and not the lark
  That sang in your ear.

ROMEO: It was the lark, announcing morning.
   No nightingale. See the light in the east.
   I must leave and live, or stay and die.

JULIET: That light is not daylight, I know it.
   So stay awhile. You do not have to go yet.

ROMEO: You know how much I want to stay.
   Let me be taken, let me be put to death.
   I am glad, if you want it so.
   I'll say the light is not the morning.
   It is the light of the moon.
   Come, death, and welcome. Juliet wills it so.
   Speak to me, Juliet. It is not yet day.

JULIET: It is, it is! Be gone, away!
   It is the lark after all. It is growing lighter.

ROMEO: The lighter it gets, the darker our woes.

(Nurse enters.)

NURSE: Your mother is coming to your room.
   It is morning. Be careful. Look about.

(Nurse exits.)

JULIET: Window, let day in, and let life out.

ROMEO: Farewell! One kiss, and I'll leave.
   (They kiss. Romeo climbs down to the garden.)

JULIET: Are you gone, my love, my friend?
   I must hear from you every day.

ROMEO: Farewell! I will send word soon.

JULIET: Do you think we shall ever meet again?

ROMEO: I doubt it not. In the future, all these
woes will be but sweet memories.

JULIET: Oh, God! I have a bad feeling about this!
I see you, there on the ground,
As one dead in the bottom of a tomb.
Either my eyesight fails, or you look pale.

ROMEO: My love, you look pale, too.
Dry sorrow drinks our blood. Farewell!

(Romeo exits.)

JULIET: Oh, Fate! Send him back soon!

(Lady Capulet enters.)

LADY CAPULET: Hello, Juliet! Are you up?

JULIET: Madam, I am not well.

LADY CAPULET: Still weeping for your cousin?
Will you wash him from his grave with tears?
Tears can't make the dead live,
So stop crying. Some grief shows love, but
Too much makes you look foolish.
I have some joyful news for you, Daughter.

JULIET: Joy is welcome in such a sad time.
What is the news, Mother?

LADY CAPULET: Well, child, your loving father
Has arranged a day of joy for you,
To help you forget your sorrow.

JULIET: What day is that?

LADY CAPULET: Child, on Thursday morning,
The gallant, young, and noble Paris
Shall make you his joyful bride.

JULIET: Oh, no, he will not! Why such hurry?
Why would I wed a man
Who has not courted me?
Tell my father that I will not marry yet—
But when I do, I swear
It shall be Romeo, whom you know I hate,
Never Paris! This is news indeed!

LADY CAPULET: Here comes your father.
Tell him yourself, and see how he takes it.

(Capulet and Nurse enter.)

CAPULET: Why are you still crying, my dear?
Wife, have you not told her the good news?

LADY CAPULET: I have, sir, but she says no.

CAPULET: What do you mean, she says no?
Does she not thank us? Is she not proud?
Does she not count her blessings that we
Have found so worthy a gentleman for her?

JULIET: I can never be proud of what I hate.
I will never marry Paris.

LADY CAPULET: What, are you mad?

JULIET: Good father, I beg you on my knees.
Listen to what I have to say.

CAPULET: Not another word, young baggage!
  I tell you—get to the church on Thursday,
  Or never again look me in the face.
  Wife, we thought we weren't blessed
  When God gave us only one child.
  Now I see that this one is one too much,
  And that we are cursed in having her!

LADY CAPULET: Your anger is too hot.

CAPULET: Hot! I am furious!
  Day and night, hour by hour,
  I have worked to find her a good match.
  Now we have found a noble gentleman,
  Good-looking, young, and honorable.
  And this wretched, whining fool says "No."
  I tell you this, Juliet:
  Go where you will. You shall not live here.
  You can beg, starve, and die in the streets.
  For, I promise, I'll never take you in.
  Think about it. I won't change my mind.

(Capulet exits.)

JULIET: Is there no pity for me?
  Oh, sweet Mother, please help me.
  Delay this marriage for a month, a week.
  Or, if you do not, make the bridal bed
  In the dim tomb where Tybalt lies.

LADY CAPULET: Quiet! I am through with you.

(Lady Capulet exits.)

JULIET: Oh, God! Oh, Nurse! What can I do?
My husband is alive. I have made my vows.
What is your advice? Tell me.

NURSE: Here it is: Romeo is banished.
He may never be able to return.
If he does, it will be in secret.
Paris is a lovely gentleman. Romeo is
A dish cloth compared to him.
You'll be happier in this second match,
For it is better than your first. Even if not,
Your first is dead—or as good as dead.
You're living here, and have no use of him.
Use your head: Marry Paris.

JULIET: Are you speaking from your heart?

NURSE: From my soul, too, or curse them both!

JULIET: You have been a real comfort.
Go and tell my mother that I am sorry
For having displeased my father.
Tell her that I have gone to Father Lawrence
To make my confession and be forgiven.

NURSE: I will. You are wise to do this.

*(**Nurse** exits.)*

JULIET *(aside)*: Old devil! Most wicked fiend!
What kind of advice was that?
She condemns Romeo with the
Same tongue she used to praise him!
She shall hear no more of my secrets.

I'll ask the friar what I should do.
If all else fails, may I have the power to die.

(**Juliet** *exits.*)

ACT 4

Scene 1

*(**Friar Lawrence** and **Paris** enter friar's cell.)*

FRIAR: The wedding is to be on Thursday, sir?
  The time is very short.

PARIS: Lord Capulet wants it that way.

FRIAR: You say you do not know Juliet's
  wishes. This isn't good. I do not like it.

PARIS: She is still weeping over Tybalt's death,
  So I have not had a chance to court her.
  Her father thinks it is dangerous
  For her to give herself over to such sorrow.
  In his wisdom, he rushes our marriage
  To stop the flow of her tears.
  If she spends less time alone, he thinks
  She will get over her grief more quickly.
  Now you know the reason for the haste.

*(**Juliet** enters Friar Lawrence's cell.)*

PARIS: Good to see you, my lady and my wife!

JULIET: That may be, sir—when I may be a wife.

PARIS: No maybe about it, love. It must be.

JULIET: What must be, shall be.

FRIAR: That is certain.

PARIS: Have you come to confess to this friar?

JULIET: To answer would be to confess to you.

PARIS: Do not deny to him that you love me.

JULIET: I will confess to you that I love him.

PARIS: So will you, I'm sure, say you love me.

JULIET: If I do, it will be worth more
To say it behind your back than to your face.
(to the friar): Are you free now, holy father?

FRIAR: I am, my daughter.
Paris, Juliet and I must talk alone now.

PARIS: I would not disturb your prayers!
Juliet, I will come for you early on Thursday.
Until then, farewell, and keep this holy
kiss. **(*Paris* kisses her and then exits.)**

JULIET: Oh, shut the door! And then
Come weep with me. I am past hope,
Past cure, past help!

FRIAR: Ah, Juliet, I already know your grief;
And it troubles me more than I can bear.
I hear you must marry Paris on Thursday.

JULIET: Do not tell me what you have heard
Unless you can tell me how to prevent it.
If, in your wisdom, you cannot give help,
I'll kill myself with this knife.

(She takes out a knife and shows it to him.)
God joined my heart and Romeo's, and
You joined our hands. And before this hand

Or my true heart is joined to another,
This knife shall slay them both.
Therefore, based on your long experience,
Give me some advice. If you cannot,
This bloody knife will do.
Do not take so long to speak. I long to die,
If you cannot offer me some remedy.

FRIAR: Hold on, daughter. I see some hope.
If you have the will to kill yourself
Rather than marry Paris,
You would probably risk a thing like death
To accomplish the same goal.
If you dare, I'll give you the remedy.

JULIET: I would leap from a tower
Rather than marry Paris!
I'd walk with thieves, or lurk with snakes.
Chain me with roaring bears, or lock me
In a tomb and cover me with bones.
I would do anything without fear or doubt
To remain an unstained wife.

FRIAR: Wait, then. Go home, be merry,
Say you will marry Paris. Tomorrow night,
When you are in bed, take this bottle
And drink the medicine that's inside.
Soon, a cold and drowsy feeling will run
Through all your veins.
Your pulse will seem to stop. No warmth,
No breath, shall show that you live. Your

Rosy color shall fade to pale ashes. Your
Body will appear stiff, stark, and cold.
This state shall continue for 42 hours.
Then, you will awake, as from a nap.
When Paris comes in the morning to
Wake you, you will seem to be dead.
They will take you to that ancient tomb
Where all the Capulets lie. In the meantime,
While you sleep, I will write to Romeo.
He shall come here, and he and I will be
With you when you wake. That very night,
    Romeo will take you from here to Mantua.
This will free you from your present problem
Unless you are afraid to go ahead with it.

JULIET: Give it to me! Do not tell me of fear!

(The friar hands her the bottle.)

FRIAR: Be patient. Go home, be strong.
I'll send a message to your husband.

JULIET: Love give me strength.
Farewell, dear father!

*(**They** exit.)*

Scene 2

*(**Lord and Lady Capulet, Nurse,** and **servants** enter a hall in Capulet's house.)*

CAPULET: Invite all the guests on this list.

*(Capulet gives list to **first servant**, who exits.)*
Servant, go and hire 20 skilled cooks.

SECOND SERVANT: You shall have no unskilled ones, sir. I'll test them by seeing if they can lick their fingers.

CAPULET: How can you test them that way?

SECOND SERVANT: Simple, sir. A bad cook will not lick his own fingers. Therefore, he that cannot lick his fingers will not be hired.

CAPULET: Go, be gone.

*(**Second servant** exits.)*

We are unprepared for this wedding.
Has my daughter gone to Friar Lawrence?

NURSE: Yes, she has, sir.

CAPULET: Well, maybe he can advise her.
She is such a stubborn, foolish girl.

NURSE: Here she comes, looking happy.

(Juliet enters.)

CAPULET: Now, my stubborn child! Where
have you been?

JULIET: Where I have learned to be sorry
For the sin of opposing you and your wishes.
Friar Lawrence told me to beg your pardon.
Forgive me, I pray you!
From now on, I shall obey you.

CAPULET: Send for Paris and tell him this:
They will marry tomorrow morning!

JULIET: I met Paris at Lawrence's cell.
I gave him as much love as I could
Without crossing the lines of modesty.

CAPULET: I am glad. This is as it should be.
(to a servant): Let me see Paris.
Yes, go, I say, and bring him here.
Our city has much to thank that friar for.

JULIET: Nurse, will you come to my room?
You can help me sort the special clothing
I will need for tomorrow.

LADY CAPULET: No, not until Thursday.
You can sort your clothing tomorrow.

CAPULET: Go, Nurse, go with her.
(to Lady Capulet): We'll have the wedding
tomorrow instead of Thursday.

*(**Juliet** and **Nurse** exit.)*

LADY CAPULET: We won't be ready tomorrow!

CAPULET: Don't worry. All will be well,
I promise you, wife. Go to Juliet.
Help her prepare. I'll stay up tonight.
I'll play the housewife for this once.
Oh, I forgot all the servants are gone!
Well, I'll go to Paris myself and prepare him
For tomorrow. My heart is light
Since our wayward girl has come back to us.

*(**Lord** and **Lady Capulet** exit.)*

Scene 3

*(**Juliet** and **Nurse** enter Juliet's room.)*

JULIET: Yes, those clothes are best.
Gentle Nurse, please leave me alone tonight.
I have need of many prayers
To move the heavens to smile on my state,
Which, as you know, is cross and full of sin.

*(**Lady Capulet** enters.)*

LADY CAPULET: Do you need my help?

JULIET: No, madam. We have done all we need.
So, please, let me now be left alone.
The nurse can sit up with you tonight,
For I am sure you have your hands full
With all this sudden business.

LADY CAPULET: Good night.
Go to bed and get some rest. You need it.

(Lady Capulet and Nurse exit.)

JULIET *(to herself)*: God knows when we shall
   meet again.
A fearful chill thrills through my veins
That almost freezes up the heat of life!
I'll call them back again to comfort me.
Nurse! But, no. What could she do here?
I must act my dismal scene alone.
Come, bottle.

(She holds up the bottle.)

What if this mixture does not work at all?
Shall I be married, then, tomorrow morning?
No! This shall prevent it. Lie yourself there.

(She lays down her dagger.)

What if the friar's medicine will kill me
To prevent his being dishonored for marrying
Me and Romeo? I fear he did, and yet
I think he did not, for he is a holy man.

I will not think such bad thoughts.
What if, when I am laid in the tomb,
I wake before Romeo comes to get me?
How frightening! Will I suffocate
On the foul air before Romeo comes?
Or, will I live on in that ancient tomb,
Where, for hundreds of years, the bones
Of all my buried ancestors are packed,
Where bloody Tybalt, just laid in the earth,
Lies rotting in his burial clothes? They say
Night spirits live there. When the living
Hear their shrieks, they go mad.
Oh, if I wake, shall I go crazy,
Surrounded with all these terrible fears?
Oh, look! I think I see my cousin's ghost
Seeking Romeo, whose sword killed him.
Stay, Tybalt, stay! Come to me, Romeo.
I drink this for you!

(She drinks the contents of the bottle and throws herself on the bed.)

Scene 4

*(**Lady Capulet** and **Nurse** enter a hall in Capulet's house.)*

LADY CAPULET: Get more spices, Nurse.

NURSE: The bakers call for dates and quinces.

*(**Capulet** enters.)*

CAPULET: Come! Stir! It is 3 o'clock already.
Take care of the baked meats.
Don't worry about the cost.

NURSE: Go, you house-husband, go.
Get to bed or you'll be sick tomorrow.

CAPULET: I have stayed up all night for
Lesser reasons and never been sick.

*(**Lady Capulet** and **Nurse** exit. **Servants** enter with logs and baskets.)*

What do you have there?

FIRST SERVANT: Things for the cook, sir, but I
don't know what.

CAPULET: Hurry! Hurry!

*(**Servants** exit.)*

My goodness, it's day! I hear Paris and
The musicians coming.

(Music plays from offstage.)

Nurse!

*(**Nurse** enters again.)*

Nurse! Go, wake Juliet! Get her dressed.
I'll go and chat with Paris. Hurry, I say!

*(**They** exit.)*

Scene 5

*(**Nurse** enters Juliet's room.)*

NURSE: Juliet! Fast asleep, I see! Sleepyhead!
What, not a word? You sleep by day,
For tonight, I bet, Paris will keep you awake.
My, my! How soundly she sleeps!
But I have to wake her. Madam, madam!
What, dressed in your clothes?
You must wake up now. Lady! Lady! Lady!
Oh, no! Help! Help! My lady is dead!
I wish I had never been born!
My lord! My lady!

*(**Lady Capulet** enters.)*

LADY CAPULET: What's all this noise?

NURSE: Oh, terrible day!

LADY CAPULET: What is the matter?

NURSE: Look, look! Oh, heavy day!

LADY CAPULET: Oh, me! Oh, me!
My child! My only life!
Wake up, or I will die with you!
Help! Help! Call for help.

*(**Capulet** enters.)*

CAPULET: For shame, bring Juliet out.
The groom awaits her.

NURSE AND LADY CAPULET: She's dead! She's dead!
Oh, curse the day!

CAPULET: Let me see her. Oh, no! She's cold.
Her blood is settled, and her joints are stiff.
Life and these lips have long been separated.
Death lies upon her like an early frost
Upon the sweetest flower of all the field.

NURSE AND LADY CAPULET: Oh, sorrowful day!
Oh, sad time!

CAPULET: Death took her to make me wail.
It ties my tongue and will not let me speak.

*(**Friar Lawrence** enters with **Paris**.)*

FRIAR: Is the bride ready to go to church?

CAPULET: Ready to go—but never to return.
Paris, my son! Death has married your
bride the night before your wedding.
There she lies, a flower picked by him.
Death is my son-in-law. Death is my heir.
He has married my daughter. I will die
And leave him all. Life, living, all is death's.

PARIS: Have I waited so long for the morning
That it gives me such a sight as this?

LADY CAPULET: Cursed, unhappy, hateful day!
The most miserable hour of all time!
My one loving child, my one joy, and
Cruel death has snatched her from my sight.

NURSE: Oh, woeful, woeful, woeful day!
Never was seen so black a day as this.

PARIS: I am tricked, divorced, and wronged
By you, hateful death! Oh, love! Oh, life!

CAPULET: Time! Why did you come now
  To murder my child!
  And with my child, my joys are buried.

FRIAR: Be still. For shame! Heaven and you
  All shared in this fair maid. Now heaven
  Has all of her, and the better it is for her.
  You wanted to see her move on in life.
  That was to be your heaven.
  And now you weep, seeing that she has
  Moved as high as heaven itself?
  Dry your tears! Lay flowers on this
  Fair body. And, as the custom is, dress her
  In her best clothes and bring her to church.
  Remember, though we cry for her,
  She's gone on to a happier place.

CAPULET: What we prepared for her wedding
  Will now be used for her funeral.
  Our instruments turn to mourning bells.
  Our wedding cheer is now a sad burial feast.
  Use bridal flowers for a funeral.
  Everything changes to the opposite.

FRIAR: Sir and madam, go in. And go, Sir Paris.
  Everyone! Follow fair Juliet to her grave.
  The heavens punished you for some ill.
  Offend them no more by crossing their will.

*(**All** exit.)*

ACT 5   Scene 1

*(**Romeo** enters a street in Mantua.)*

ROMEO: If I can trust my dreams,
They tell me some joyful news is coming.
My heart is light. All day, a happy spirit
Has lifted me up with cheerful thoughts.

*(**Balthasar** enters.)*

News from Verona! Hello, Balthasar!
How is my Juliet? I ask you that again,
For nothing can be bad if she is well.

BALTHASAR: Then she is well, nothing is bad.
Her body sleeps in the Capulet tomb,
And her soul is with the angels.
Oh, pardon me for bringing this bad news.

ROMEO: Is it true? Then I defy you, stars!
Hire some horses. I will leave here tonight!

BALTHASAR: I beg you, sir, be patient.
You look pale and wild.
It would be dangerous to leave like this.

ROMEO: No, you are wrong. Do as I ask.
I'll be with you right away.

*(**Balthasar** exits.)*

ROMEO: Well, Juliet, I will lie with you
   tonight.
   How will I do it?
   Ah! I remember a poor druggist
   Who lives around here. He wears
   Tattered clothes and looks hungry.
   As I remember, this should be the house.
   Being a holiday, his shop is shut.
   (knocking on the door): Hello? Druggist!

*(**Druggist** enters.)*

DRUGGIST: Who calls so loud?

ROMEO: Come here. I see that you are poor.
   Here are 40 gold coins. Let me have
   An ounce of poison—something
   That will flow through all the veins
   And make the life-weary taker fall dead
   As fast as gunpowder fires a cannon.

DRUGGIST: I have such deadly drugs,
   But Mantua's law means death to
      anyone who sells them.

ROMEO: Are you so afraid to die?
   Hunger shows in your cheeks.
   Need and misery flow in your eyes.
   Poverty hangs on your back.
   The world has no law to make you rich.
   Break the law, and take this gold.

DRUGGIST: My poverty, not my will, says yes.

(Druggist hands Romeo the poison.)

DRUGGIST: Put this in any liquid you wish,
And drink it. Even if you are as strong
As 20 men, it will kill you right away.

ROMEO: Here is your gold. Money is even a
worse poison to men's souls.
It does more murders in this evil world,
Than this poison that you may not sell.
Farewell. Buy food and make yourself well.

Scene 2

*(**Friar John** enters Friar Lawrence's cell.)*

FRIAR JOHN: Hello? Father Lawrence?

*(**Friar Lawrence** enters.)*

FRIAR LAWRENCE: That sounds like Friar John.
Welcome back. What did Romeo say?
Or did he write a letter for me?

FRIAR JOHN: No. Before I left, I went to find
Another brother to go with me.
He was here in this city, visiting the sick.
The health inspectors of the town thought
The house was infected by the plague.
So they sealed up the doors and would not
Let us leave. I was not able to go to Mantua.

FRIAR LAWRENCE: Who delivered my letter?

FRIAR JOHN: I could not send it—nor could I
Get a messenger to bring it back to you.
Everyone was afraid of the plague.
Here is your letter.

FRIAR LAWRENCE: Oh, no! The letter was
Very important. By not delivering it,
We may cause much damage!
Friar John, go and get me a crowbar!
Bring it straight to my cell.

*(**Friar John** exits.)*

FRIAR LAWRENCE: I must go to the tomb alone.
Within three hours the fair Juliet will wake.
She will be angry with me for not
Getting the message to Romeo.
But I will write again to Mantua, and
Keep her in my cell until Romeo comes.
Poor living girl, in a dead man's tomb!

*(**Friar Lawrence** exits.)*

Scene 3

*(**Paris** and his **servant** enter the churchyard around the Capulet tomb. The servant carries flowers and a torch.)*

PARIS: Give me the torch and stand there.
No, put it out. I don't want to be seen.

Wait over there by those yew trees.
If you hear anyone coming, whistle to me.
Give me those flowers. Do as I say. Go!

(Servant exits.)

PARIS: Sweet Juliet. Every night, I shall bring
Flowers here and water them with tears.

(Servant whistles.)

The boy warns that someone is coming!
Who wanders this way tonight
To disturb my prayers for sweet Juliet?
Hide me, night, for awhile. *(He hides.)*

*(**Romeo** enters with **Balthasar**, who carries a torch and tools.)*

ROMEO: Give me the axe and the crowbar.
Here, take this letter to my father tomorrow.
Give me the light. Now go!
If you return to peek at what I intend to do,
I promise I will tear you limb from limb
And scatter you all over the churchyard!
I am as wild as a savage, more fierce
Than hungry tigers or the roaring sea.

BALTHASAR: I will leave, sir.

ROMEO: You show me true friendship.
Live, prosper, and farewell, good fellow.

BALTHASAR *(aside)***:** Even so, I'll hide nearby.
I fear his looks and doubt his plans.
(He hides.)

ROMEO: You hateful tomb, you womb of death,
You have gorged yourself
With the dearest morsel of the earth!
Thus, I force your rotten jaws to open.

(He breaks open the door of the tomb.)
In spite, I'll cram you with more food!

PARIS: It is that banished proud Montague
Who murdered my love's cousin.
Some say she died of grief over it.
He has come here to do some shame
To the dead bodies. I will stop him.

(Paris comes out of hiding.)
Stop your unholy work, evil Montague!
Can you get greater revenge than death?
You villain, I arrest you!
Come with me, for you must die.

ROMEO: Indeed I must. That's why I came here.
Gentle sir, do not tempt a desperate man.
Fly from here and leave me.
Think about these dead and be afraid.
I beg you, do not make me angry!
By heaven, I love you better than myself,
For I come here armed against myself.

PARIS: I will ignore your nonsense.
I am arresting you as an outlaw here!

ROMEO: Will you provoke me? Then fight, boy!

*(They fight with swords. Paris's **servant** enters.)*

88

SERVANT: Oh, lord! I will go call the guards.

*(**Servant** exits.)*

PARIS *(falling to the ground)*: Oh, I am slain!
If you have any mercy,
Open the tomb, and lay me with Juliet.

*(**Paris** dies.)*

ROMEO: I promise, I will. Let me see your face.

(Romeo looks more closely at Paris.)

Mercutio's relative! The noble Paris!
What did Balthasar say, as we rode here from
    Mantua? I think he told me that Paris
Was supposed to marry Juliet.
Didn't he say so? Or did I dream it?
Or have I gone mad?

(He takes Paris's hand.)

Oh, give me your hand, gentle Paris.
Both of our stories are told
In misfortune's book.
I'll bury you in a splendid grave.
A grave? Oh, no, it is rather a lantern,
For here lies Juliet. Her beauty makes
This tomb a banquet hall full of light.
Lie here, Paris, buried by another dead man.

(Romeo lays Paris in the tomb, near Juliet.)

Oh, my love, my wife! Death, which has
Sucked the honey of your breath,

Has had no power yet upon your beauty.
Tybalt, do you lie there in your bloody sheet?
Oh, what better thing can I do for you
  than to
Kill the one who cut your youth in two?
Forgive me, cousin! Ah, dear Juliet,
Why are you still so beautiful? Is it that
Death is in love with you, and that he keeps
You here in the dark to be his bride?
For fear of that, I still will stay with you, and
Never again leave this palace of dim night.
Come, bitter poison!
Pilot my sick and weary ship onto the rocks!
Here's to my love! *(He drinks the poison.)*
Oh, honest druggist, your drugs are quick.
Thus, with a kiss, I die.

*(Romeo kisses Juliet and dies. At the other end of the churchyard, **Friar Lawrence** enters carrying a lantern, a crowbar, and a shovel.)*

FRIAR: I must hurry! Oh! Who's there?

BALTHASAR: A friend who knows you well.

FRIAR: Bless you! Tell me, my good friend,
    What torch is over there, lending its light
    To worms and eyeless skulls? I see
    It burns in the Capulets' tomb.

BALTHASAR: My master is there.

FRIAR: Who is he?

BALTHASAR: Romeo.

FRIAR: How long has he been there?

BALTHASAR: For half an hour.

FRIAR: Go with me to the tomb.

BALTHASAR: I dare not, sir. My master thinks
   I went home. He threatened to kill me
      if I stayed.

FRIAR: Stay here then. I'll go alone.
   I fear some terrible thing has happened.

FRIAR (going into the tomb): Romeo!
   What blood is this that stains this stony door?
   Why do these bloody swords lie here
   In this place of peace? Romeo! You are pale!
   Who else? Paris, too? Covered in blood?
   What an unkind hour! The lady moves.

JULIET (waking up): Oh, Friar!
   Where is my lord? Where is my Romeo?

(A noise is heard from offstage.)

FRIAR: I hear a noise. Lady, come from this nest
   Of death, decay, and unnatural sleep.
   Your dear husband lies dead, and Paris, too.
   Come, I'll hide you with some holy nuns.
   Do not stay to ask why. Someone is coming.
   Come and go, good Juliet.

(More noise is heard.)

   I dare not stay any longer.

JULIET: Go, get away! I will not leave.

(Friar Lawrence exits.)

> What's this? A cup in my true love's hand?
> Poison, I see, has taken his life. Romeo!
> You drank it all. No friendly drop for me?
> I will kiss your lips. Perhaps some poison
> Still remains there to kill me, too.
> (She kisses him.) Your lips are warm!

FIRST GUARD (offstage)**:** Lead on. Which way?

JULIET: Noise? I'll be brief. Oh, happy dagger!

(She takes Romeo's dagger and points it toward her heart.)

> My body is your sheath. Enter, and let me die.

(She stabs herself, falls on Romeo's body, and dies. **Guards** enter, with Paris's **servant**.)

FIRST GUARD: The ground is bloody here.
> Go, some of you! Catch whoever you can.

(Some of the **guards** exit.)

> Pitiful sight! Here lies Paris dead,
> And Juliet bleeding, yet still warm. But
> She was buried here two days ago!
> Go, tell the Prince! Run to the Capulets!
> Wake up the Montagues!

(More guards exit. **Other guards** enter, with **Balthasar.**)

SECOND GUARD: Here's Romeo's servant.
   We found him in the churchyard.

FIRST GUARD: Hold him for the Prince.

*(**More guards** enter, with **Friar Lawrence**.)*

THIRD GUARD: Here is a friar that trembles,
   Sighs, and weeps. We took these tools
   From him as he was leaving the churchyard.

FIRST GUARD: How strange! Hold the friar, too.

*(The **Prince, Lord and Lady Capulet**, and **servants** enter.)*

PRINCE: What is going on here,
   That disturbs our morning's rest?

FIRST GUARD: Here lies Paris, dead.
   And Romeo dead. And Juliet, dead
      before—yet now warm and newly killed.

PRINCE: Find out how these murders happened!

FIRST GUARD: This friar and Romeo's servant
   Had tools that can open the tombs.

CAPULET: Oh, wife! Our daughter bleeds!
   There is a Montague dagger in her heart.

LADY CAPULET: Oh, my! This sight is like
   A bell, warning of my own death.

*(**Montague** and **others** enter.)*

PRINCE: Come, Montague, see your son.

MONTAGUE: Prince, my wife died last night.
   Grief over my son's exile stopped her breath.

What further woe torments my old age?

PRINCE: Look, and you will see.

MONTAGUE: Romeo! What poor manners—
To go before your father to a grave!

PRINCE: Contain your grief and outrage
Until we find out what happened here.
Bring forth the suspects.

FRIAR: I can tell you what happened here.
Romeo, lying there dead,
Was Juliet's husband. And she, there dead,
Was Romeo's faithful wife. I married them
On the day of Tybalt's death,
Which banished the groom from this city.
Juliet pined for Romeo—not for Tybalt.
To remove her grief, her parents
Arranged for her to marry Paris.
Then she came to me, with wild looks,
And begged me to find some way
To save her from this second marriage,
Or she would kill herself in my cell!
So I gave her a sleeping potion, which
Took effect as I planned. It made her
Appear to be dead. Then I wrote to Romeo
Saying he should come here tonight
To take her from her borrowed grave
As soon as she awakened.
But he who took my letter, Friar John,
Was not able to deliver it. Next I came,

All alone, at the time she was to awaken.
I wanted to take her from the tomb and hide
Her in my cell until I could send for Romeo.
But when I got here, just before her awaking,
I found the noble Paris and true Romeo dead.
She woke, and I begged her to go with me.
But then a noise scared me from the tomb.
In her grief, she would not go with me—
And, as it seems, did violence on herself.
If you find that this is all my fault,
Let my old life be sacrificed.
Take it before its time, according to the law.

PRINCE: We still think of you as a holy man.
What can Romeo's servant say about this?

BALTHASAR: I brought my master news of
Juliet's death. Then he hurried here from
   Mantua. He gave me a letter for his father,
And threatened to kill me if I didn't leave.

PRINCE: Give me the letter. I will look at it.
Where is Paris's servant, who called
For the guards? Why was your master here?

SERVANT: He came with flowers for his lady.
He told me to stand back, so I did.
Someone came with a light to open the tomb.
Soon, my master drew his sword on him,
So I ran away to call the guards.

PRINCE: This letter supports the friar's words.
It speaks of their love, the news of her death.

And he writes that he bought some poison.
He came here to die and to lie with Juliet.
Where are the enemies? Capulet! Montague!
See what your hate has done.
Heaven tried to kill your anger with love!
And I, for winking at your fighting,
Have lost two relatives. All are punished.

CAPULET: Montague, give me your hand.
Let this be my daughter's wedding dowry.
I can ask for no more.

MONTAGUE: But I can give you more.
I will raise her statue in pure gold.
As long as Verona's name is known,
There will be no one as honored
As the true and faithful Juliet.

CAPULET: I will do the same for Romeo,
And have him lie beside her.
Poor sacrifices of our hate!

PRINCE: A gloomy peace this morning brings.
The sun, in sorrow, will not show its face.
Go! We'll talk more of these sad things.
Some will be pardoned, and some
    punished.
For never was a story more full of woe
Than this tale of Juliet and Romeo.

*(**All** exit.)*